T0057457

The
Complete Illustrated
Guide to
Zen

The
Complete Illustrated
Guide to
Zen

Seigaku Amato

Wisdom

Wisdom Publications
199 Elm Street
Somerville, MA 02144 USA
wisdomexperience.org

© 2021 Seigaku Amato
All rights reserved.

No part of this book may be reproduced in any form or by any means,
electronic or mechanical, including photography, recording, or by any
information storage and retrieval system or technologies now known or
later developed, without permission in writing from the publisher.

Library of Congress Cataloging-in-Publication Data
Names: Amato, Seigaku, author.
Title: The complete illustrated guide to Zen / Seigaku Amato.
Description: Somerville, MA, USA: Wisdom Publications, 2021.
Identifiers: LCCN 2020030279 (print) | LCCN 2020030280 (ebook) |
    ISBN 9781614295716 | ISBN 9781614295952 (ebook)
Subjects: LCSH: Sotoshu. | Zen Buddhism.
Classification: LCC BQ9415.6 .A63 2021 (print) | LCC BQ9415.6 (ebook) |
    DDC 294.3/927—dc23
LC record available at https://lccn.loc.gov/2020030279
LC ebook record available at https://lccn.loc.gov/2020030280

ISBN 978-1-61429-571-6   ebook ISBN 978-1-61429-595-2

25 24 23 22 21
5 4 3 2

Artwork and design by Seigaku Amato.

Printed on acid-free paper that meets the guidelines for permanence
and durability of the Production Guidelines for Book Longevity of the
Council on Library Resources.

Printed in the United States of America.

With nine bows of gratitude
to Gyokei Yokoyama and Taimei
Ohara. To all my teachers past,
present, and future.

Contents

Introduction

This book is intended as a guide for the individual practicing Soto Zen Buddhism. Whether you are taking the first step on your journey, ordaining as a priest, or leading a practice community, the goal of this work is to be a resource for the practice of Soto Zen Buddhism. In the United States there are a variety of lineages of Soto Zen, and they each have their own way of expressing the forms or ceremony, zazen, work, and liturgy, as they were handed down from teacher to student. There is no right or wrong way to practice the forms of Zen within each tradition. Each lineage has its own history, tradition, and emphasis on important sutras, chants, and liturgical forms.

As Soto Zen was transmitted to the United States primarily by priests from either Eihei-ji or Soji-ji, the two head monasteries of Soto Zen in Japan, it can be argued that Western Soto Zen gives the impression that the monastic tradition in Japan is the "correct" expression of Soto Zen.

However, as teachers such as Shunryu Suzuki, Taizan Maezumi, Dainin Katagiri, and Kobun Chino Otogawa began to plant firm roots of Soto Zen in America, it began to take on unique expressions that are relevant to the United States. These changes include an emphasis on the practice of zazen by lay Buddhists, lay leadership, and establishment of priest training centers in the United States.

One major similarity between Soto Zen Buddhism in the United States and Japan is that clergy are not required to be celibate. In both countries priests come from a wide variety of backgrounds, from living in an apartment with their partners and children to being celibate in a monastery. This fact may come as a shock to some people, as the typical vision of Zen clergy is the celibate Buddhist monk. No matter what particular lineage you may practice in, it is important that you follow the forms of the community with which you are practicing. The right form is the form that that particular community is following. It is in line with the philosophy of Zen to be fluid and accept circumstances as they are, when it is appropriate.

A Brief History

Soto Zen is a branch of Buddhism in the Mahayana tradition. Mahayana is also called the "great vehicle," and its emphasis is on the practice of a bodhisattva. A bodhisattva is a being who has a deep experiential knowledge of Buddhadharma and yet remains in the world of samsara, or suffering, to help all living beings until they too can pass into nirvana.

The Mahayana is further subdivided into the exoteric and esoteric schools. The Zen, Nichiren, and Jodo-shinshu sects of Buddhism are in the exoteric tradition and are some of the most popular. The Shingon and Tendai are among the esoteric schools. In the exoteric sects the teachings are openly practiced by adherents, and nothing is hidden from the uninitiated.

On the other hand, the esoteric branch has very strict practices regarding who gets to learn certain mantras, mudras, and meditation techniques, and when they get to learn them. There is considerably less written about these esoteric schools, as the information is guarded and transmitted secretly from a master to a disciple.

12

All of these branches of Buddhism trace their roots back to the teachings of Shakyamuni Buddha. The Soto sect of Zen has been handed down from teacher to disciple in a spreading network of roots from generation to generation and country to country.

Original teacher Shakyamuni Buddha

Saicho of Tendai

Kukai of Shingon

Honen of Jodo

Shinran of Jodoshin

Nichiren of Nichiren

Dogen of Soto

The Soto lineage remained the same from temple to temple up until roughly Keizan Zenji (1268–1325). Keizan is considered the second founder of Soto Zen in Japan as he was a great reformer and Soto Zen was popularized under his direction. Since Keizan many teachers have transmitted the Dharma, and each temple has its own lineage in relation to the practice of Soto Zen. All Soto Zen shares the two founders Dogen and Keizan. Dogen (1200–1253) was the priest who traveled to China in search of the true Dharma to answer his fundamental question: If we are all enlightened from the start, then what is the point of practicing Buddhism?

Shakyamuni Buddha

Keizan Zenji

Dogen Zenji

Dogen found his answer with his teacher, Tendo Nyojo, while practicing in the mountains of China. Dogen taught that practice and enlightenment are not two separate things, but one. We don't practice to become enlightened, but practice is itself the expression of enlightenment. Dogen then took the practice of Soto Zen back with him to Japan and began to teach monks the practice of Shikantaza, or just sitting.

Dogen taught practice-enlightenment to many people but then began to focus on training monks. He emphasized strict adherence to monastic codes of conduct and maintaining the monastic schedule of Eihei-ji, the first training monastery of Soto Zen in Japan. This meant that the teachings were not permeating the everyday lives of the laity. Soto Zen was behind a monastery door that was accessible only to those who were granted permission to train in the monastery.

Dogen wrote a great deal on the practice of Soto Zen, and his essays have been compiled in many different languages. Such works as the *Shobogenzo*, or True Dharma Eye, are extensive commentaries and instructions on the Zen way. To this day the Fukanzazengi, or Universal Recommendation for Zazen, is chanted daily in Soto Zen temples, monasteries, and centers throughout the world.

During Keizan's life Soto Zen began to flourish in the lives of the laity and then took strong hold to become what is now the contemporary Soto Zen. Keizan was supportive of the lay practice of Soto Zen, gave the laity the Bodhisattva precepts in the Jukai ceremony, and encouraged the practice to spread in their daily lives.

This is in great contrast to the approach of the monastic-oriented training of Dogen Zenji. Keizan was also devoted to the congregations of the temples and monasteries of Soto Zen. He focused on serving the needs of the community in ways that a monastic education did not prioritize, such as performing funerals, weddings, and memorials and spreading the teaching to the daily lives of all people, regardless of class and circumstance.

Keizan founded Soji-ji monastery, and this became just as influential in Soto Zen as Dogen's founding of Eihei-ji. Keizan wrote his own works in relation to the study and practice of Soto Zen. The most popular works of Keizan are the *Zazen Yojinki*, or Points to Watch in Zazen, and the *Denkoroku*, or Transmission of the Light. The *Denkoroku* is an in-depth history of the Soto Zen ancestors from Shakyamuni Buddha all the way down to the fifty-second ancestor in Japan, Koun Ejo. The *Denkoroku* covers brief historical contexts of the ancestors, their spiritual struggle, and what their kensho, or enlightening experiences, were.

Buddhas and Bodhisattvas

There are many buddhas and bodhisattvas to be discussed in the Zen tradition. There are also a number of other deities that belong to neither of the previous groups but, nonetheless, maintain a very important position within the network of deities. For each individual deity there also can be many forms to convey subtle aspects of their practice. In this chapter, the focus is on the basic buddhas, bodhisattvas, and Fudo Myo-o, as he is a very popular deity in Zen.

Amida Buddha surrounded by a bodhisattva and heavenly beings.

Visually standing in stark contrast to the heavenly beings is the Nio, above. The Nio are a pair of protector dieties that guard the gates of temples to protect the Dharma.

Here is another class of deity known as a Myo-o, or wisdom king. This particular Myo-o is Aizen Myo-o, who transforms lust into wisdom through practice. Before we get too far into this list, first we are going to cover the different buddhas who are venerated and what they represent.

Shakyamuni Buddha

Shakyamuni Buddha is the historical Buddha who lived in the world. His name was Siddhartha Gautama, and he was born into a royal family in Kapilavastu. Siddhartha was of the Shakya tribe, and his parents were King Suddhodana and Queen Maha Maya. Gautama left his home and searched for an end to the suffering we experience in life. He saw that all things are subject to birth, old age, disease, and death.

No lasting happiness can be found that depends on compounded things. Gautama set out to find a path out of suffering. After many years of asceticism he was still unable to find the answers he was desperately seeking. After abandoning asceticism Gautama began to sit zazen. He sat for seven days, and at the end of this period he became enlightened. Upon enlightenment Buddha saw the interdependence of all things. He saw that all phenomena are inherently empty and void of an eternal self. Gautama experienced the simultaneous enlightenment of "I and all beings" and became Shakyamuni Buddha. Shakyamuni taught that the path to enlightenment resided in the middle way, four noble truths, and eightfold path. The middle way is the avoidance of self-indulgence and asceticism. For our mental and physical health, we need food, clothing, and shelter. We need to take food in moderation to support our bodies to practice the Dharma. Clothing and shelter keep us warm or cool to sit zazen throughout the seasons. When our intake of food is not balanced, we can become sick. When we are too attached to our clothing, we desire new and better garments. Being too attached to a nice home or staying indoors too long is not good for our mental health.

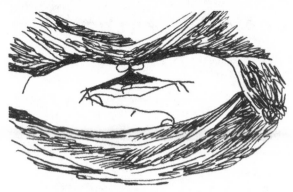

There are different mudras that are associated with Shakyamuni Buddha. This helps to identify which buddha is sitting on the altar. Shakyamuni is usually depicted seated in the full lotus posture on a lotus throne with his hands resting in the cosmic mudra, also called hokkai-join.

When Shakyamuni is not seated with hands in the hokkai-join, you will find him with his left hand in his lap and his right hand, palm down, touching the earth in front of him. This is called the earth witnessing mudra. This mudra comes from the moment when Shakyamuni Buddha called on the earth to witness his enlightenment during zazen on December 8, the day of his enlightenment.

The Four Noble Truths

Shakyamuni Buddha taught the four noble truths as a framework for understanding our suffering.

#1. The truth of suffering as part of conditioned existence.

We are born into the world and quickly develop likes and dislikes. We feel pain, fear, confusion, and many other negative emotions. Suffering can be both subtle and dramatic.

Being with those we don't like.

Experiencing physical pain, like a toothache.

Enduring the death of a loved one.

#2. The truth that suffering has a cause.

We create our own suffering through our desire. We want things we can't have, and we reach for them. This creates suffering. We have things we don't want and push them away. This too creates suffering.

Having the understanding that I am entirely separate from you creates further suffering. When we see ourselves as separate from someone, we create a story that there is someone out there that is bothering "me." In the "Sandokai," or The Harmony of Relative and Absolute, a text chanted daily in Soto Zen temples, we are reminded that there are relative and absolute truths. The relative truth is that you and I are different. The absolute truth is that you and I are of the same makeup, the four elements and five skandhas, which are material form, feeling, perception, volition, and consciousness. Our lack of understanding that all things are interdependent leads to a false sense of self. If I see things outside myself, then I will want or reject them. I want good experiences, not bad experiences. Yet, it can be difficult to enjoy good experiences too.

"Going shopping for new shoes is great! Eating cake is great! I should be running more. Cake is bad for me. Running is hard."

#3. The truth that there is an end to suffering.

Beyond grasping, aversion, and the illusion of control, there is peace to be found in understanding the selfless nature of all phenomena. We can discover that nothing is lacking and there is nothing to push away. There are no walls to hold us in, and we can experience all phenomena as a seamless state of mind. Nothing is born and nothing truly dies, so there is nothing to cling to. No birth to desire and no death to be avoided.

#4. The truth of the path that leads out of suffering.

The eightfold path is:

Proper view—seeing things as they truly are.

Proper thought—thinking in accord with things as they are.

Proper speech—refraining from harmful speech.

Proper action—acting in accord with the precepts.

Proper livelihood—making our living in a way that limits suffering.

Proper effort—continuing on the path to enlightenment.

Proper mindfulness—being aware of the contents of our thoughts.

Proper meditation—practicing meditation with our bodies and minds.

Dainichi Nyorai
The Cosmic Buddha

Dainichi Nyorai is the Cosmic Buddha. In Sanskrit, Dainichi's name is Mahavairocana Buddha, meaning Great Sun Buddha. This is another way to say Cosmic Buddha, as this buddha represents the center of the cosmos that everything revolves around. Dainichi is often depicted with hands in the chi ken-in mudra, or the knowledge fist mudra.

This mudra represents internal focus and is said to bring about the concentration of mind and body. Sometimes Dainichi appears in iconography with other buddhas adorning the mandala. Other times Dainichi is depicted as a king with a crown and the adornments more commonly associated with a bodhisattva, as seen to the left. Dainichi is not as popularly displayed in Zen temples and centers, but he is commonly referred to as Birushana, or Vairochana, the Cosmic Buddha. Dainichi's name is invoked during the mealtime sutra recitations.

Yakushi Nyorai
The Medicine Buddha

Yakushi Nyorai is the buddha associated with healing. The name of this buddha in Sanskrit is Bhaisajyaguru Tathagata, meaning
master of medicine or healing. In the
left hand of Yakushi is a small jar of
medicine to provide relief to those
suffering from afflictions of the
mind and body. The right hand of
Yakushi is held up in the mudra to
ease fear. Together these mudras
display the message not to be afraid
and come closer to take the medicine of the Dharma to relieve your
suffering.

Yakushi Nyorai can be venerated
by anyone for any reason, but is
most popularly venerated
by those suffering from
illness, injury, or malnu-
trition. A good way to
practice with Yakushi Nyorai is to chant the mantra
"On koro koro sendari
matougi sowaka," which is a
petition to bring about healing. You can also gift an image of
Yakushi Nyorai to an injured or ill loved
one. The serene image may just bring
about a calming effect. Another way
of practicing with Yakushi Nyorai would be to place an image of Yakushi in a
healing place such as a medicine cabinet or clinic, or, if one is a medical practitioner, to practice recitation of the Yakushi mantra before treating patients.

Fudo Myo-o
The Immovable One

Fudo Myo-o, whose name in Sanskrit is Acala Vidyaraja, is not considered to be a buddha or bodhisattva. Fudo is a Myo-o, or "wisdom king." The Myo-o are wrathful deities that represent the overcoming of passions through practice of the Dharma. Fudo is the most popular Myo-o, depicted with a snarling gaze and with a devil-subduing sword in the right hand that cuts through ignorance. In his left hand is a rope that snares the demons of greed, hate, and delusion. Fudo Myo-o sits immovable on a slab of rock anchored in place, displaying the determination to train the self in Buddhism. The fire blazes around Fudo, representing the purifying and burning away of worldly desires.

Amida Nyorai
The Buddha of Infinite Life and Light

Amida is generally venerated most in the Jodo Shinshu, or Pure Land sect of Buddhism. This buddha looks very much like depictions of Shakyamuni Buddha and is often confused with Shakyamuni in the West. One major tell that you are looking at Amida and not Shakyamuni is the mudra. When seated, Amida has hands in the jo-in, or mudra similar to Shakyamuni, but the index fingers and thumbs on each hand make a circle. When standing, Amida will usually have hands in segan semui-in mudra, as depicted here. The practice of chanting the Nembutsu, "Namu Amida Butsu," is practiced in the Jodo Shinshu and Jodo Shu schools of Buddhism. By chanting the Nembutsu, the chanter can attain rebirth in Amida Buddha's Western Pure Land, where conditions are easier for enlightenment. This is considered "relying on the other power," or power of Amida Buddha's vow to save all beings in all walks of life. When we are on our deathbed, by chanting the Nembutsu with pure faith, Amida Buddha with twenty-five bodhisattva attendants will greet us and lead us to the Pure Land. Often in Zen it is believed that Amida Buddha's Pure Land is no other place than this very world we live in right here and now.

Miroku Bosatsu
The Buddha to Be

Miroku Bosatsu, also called Maitreya Bodhisattva in Sanskrit, is the buddha that is to come. Miroku resides in the Tushita heaven as a bodhisattva. As all things are impermanent, there is said to be three eras that Buddhism is practiced in. The first age is the age of Shakyamuni Buddha teaching directly. The second is what is taught by direct disciples of Shakyamuni. The third age is the degenerate age when Buddhism has changed so much that it is no longer the practice of Buddhism. It is stated that this is the age when Miroku Bodhisattva will be born on earth as a buddha to revive the Buddhist teachings, when they have faded and fallen out of practice. Miroku can be represented as either a buddha or a bodhisattva, as depicted to the right. With each person who begins to practice the Dharma, Miroku emerges into the world. During the mealtime sutra recitation in Zen temples, Miroku is listed as one of the names of the ten buddhas, as Maitreya of Future Birth.

Jizo Bodhisattva

Earth Womb Bodhisattva

Jizo Bodhisattva, or Ksitigarbha, is the only bodhisattva that is represented in the form of a priest. In Jizo's right hand is the traveling staff of a Buddhist priest. The staff has six iron rings, one for each of the realms of being in the Buddhist universe: hell, hungry ghosts, animals, humans, asuras, and heaven. Jizo travels the six realms in order to relieve the suffering of all sentient beings in each realm. This is the reason that Jizo appears as a priest, as priests make the vow to save all sentient beings in all worlds. In Jizo's left hand is the mani hoju, or cintamani jewel.

This jewel fulfills wishes, grants the wisdom of the buddhas, gives blessings, and removes suffering. Jizo is venerated particularly by travelers and by mothers and fathers who have lost children and is often associated with protecting pets. It is not uncommon to see statues of Jizo wearing children's hats and bibs, as these are offerings from parents who are grieving the loss of a child.

Kannon Bodhisattva
Regarder of the Cries of the World

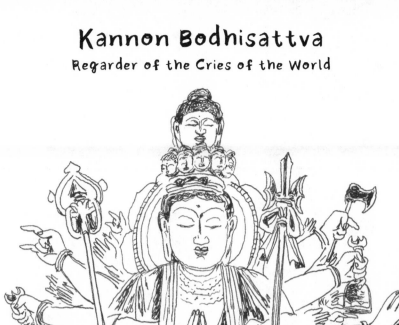

Kannon Bodhisattva, also called Avalokitesvara in Sanskrit, is the bodhisattva who represents great compassion. Kannon's name means "One Who Hears All." There are many forms of Kannon in Buddhist iconography, depending on the forms of suffering that Kannon can address. There are wrathful images of Kannon such as Bato Kannon, or Horse-head Kannon, who is a protector; Juichi men Kannon, the eleven-headed Kannon; and the Senju Kannon, the thousand-armed Kannon, as depicted here. No matter the depiction of Kannon, the theme is the same; the bodhisattva eases suffering with vast and limitless compassion.

Fugen Bodhisattva
Gentle Glory Bodhisattva

Fugen Bodhisattva, called Samanta-bhadra in Sanskrit, is the bodhisat-tva associated with right conduct and following the precepts. Fugen is often shown holding a lotus, representing the true nature of humankind that can bloom from the mud of delusion. When not holding a lotus, Fugen is seen with hands in gassho, as depicted here, riding a six-tusked elephant repre-senting freedom from attachment to the six senses and overcoming obstacles. Fugen is usually with Monju, illustrating the pairing of zazen and precepts practice with wisdom of the enlightened mind.

Monju Bodhisattva
Great Conduct Bodhisattva

Monju, or Manjusri in Sanskrit, is shown here holding a sutra in the left hand, representing the wisdom of Dharma, and a sword in the right hand for cutting away delusion. Monju is rep-resented riding a lion symbol-izing the ability to overcome obstacles with the practice of Buddhadharma. Monju is the Bodhisattva of Wisdom and the enlightened mind through the practice of Buddhism.

Butsudan
The Buddhist Altar

In this chapter we are going to discuss the significance of the butsudan, or Buddhist home altar. It is important to create a space that is devoted to practicing the Buddhadharma. The space can be as elaborate or as simple as you desire. We are going to cover how to set up a butsudan and how to practice with one.

Typically the average Buddhist altar consists of the main image of a buddha or bodhisattva. Many home altars also contain the memorial tablets of one's deceased loved ones. Offerings are made not only to Buddha, but also to one's ancestors. This is very similar to bringing flowers to a memorial site or grave. The offerings made at the altar are incense, candles, flowers, fruit, and water or tea.

Every butsudan has a main image of veneration. Many different buddhas and bodhisattvas exist and represent many aspects of the Dharma. There are many aspects to Buddha's teaching, and a representational image can help to inspire the quality of a particular teaching. This is like a visual shorthand language. Many people find an affinity to a specific image of a buddha or bodhisattva. Finding a deity or image that resonates with you can help your practice.

Most often the main object of veneration in Zen Buddhism is Shakyamuni Buddha sitting in the zazen posture, but any buddha or bodhisattva will work. Whatever figure is chosen for the butsudan, the significance stays the same. The image in the butsudan is not there to be worshipped, but to raise up the Buddha mind that it represents. It is inspiring to look at such an image of serenity and limitless compassion. We practice in order to make ourselves such a representation in daily life.

A good way to make a spiritual connection with making offerings on the butsudan is to understand the significance of the offerings. Here is a list of the main offerings and what they represent. Candles offer light to follow the Dharma. In the darkness of ignorance, a candle brightens the way to the other shore of nirvana. Incense permeates all areas in space just as the Dharma does.

Incense is a purifying substance that washes away the stench of greed, hate, and delusion. The fragrance is what is being offered to Buddha, so if smoke is diffi-cult for you, there is smokeless incense that can be used. Flowers illustrate the truth of impermanence. The beautiful offerings of flowers are pleasing to look at and show the time of the season that the offer-ings are being made. Flowers in spring, greenery in the summer, red maple leaves in the fall, and pine branches in the winter show us the beauty of the stages of life. The present moment is represented on the butsudan. Tea and food sustain us in our practice and are given out of gratitude for the compassion and blessings of the Buddha, ances-tors, and teachers who spread the Dharma.

It may seem strange to leave food on the butsudan because the Buddha is not going to eat it, but it is an offering of food to the Buddha, Dharma, and Sangha before we eat our own meal. The offering should be made with the same attitude as we offer a guest refreshments and a place to sit down before we serve ourselves.

The food that is offered on the butsudan won't be wasted, as it will be taken down from the altar and eaten by families, priests, spirits, or pets. Along with what is offered on a butsudan, there are forms to follow when practicing with one. The forms convey a sense of gratitude and respect to the three treasures of Buddha, Dharma, and Sangha.

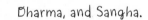

The forms used when practicing with a home altar are another way of practicing Buddhadharma, just like when we sit zazen and walk in kinhin. The forms can range from very elaborate, such as prostrations, incense offerings, and chanting, to something as simple as a gassho and ringing of a bell. In the monastery forms are very elaborate and have been adapted to different sanghas to fit with the culture of the center. When practicing at home, changing certain forms is an excellent way to establish family or personal traditions.

Praticing at home with a butsudan is a great way to commit to daily practice. One of the simplest ways to practice with a home altar is, first thing in the morning when you wake up, to go to the butsudan and light a stick of incense.

Touching the incense to your forehead, say, "Namu kie butsu, namu kie ho, namu kie so," or "Being one with Buddha, being one with Dharma, being one with Sangha." After reciting the three refuges, place the incense in the bowl and then strike the bell and place your hands in gassho, take a few deep breaths, and start your everyday routine. Throughout the day, the merit of your practice with a home altar along with your zazen practice will bring you focus, peace, and stability.

For a more elaborate service, the same routine can be followed
with the addition of sanpai, or three prostrations. Prostrations begin with the hands in gassho, bowing
forward onto the knees, and then putting
your forehead on the floor and raising
the hands, palms up, above your ears.
This is raising the Buddha mind up
above that of your ego.

Chanting the Maka Hannya Haramita Shin Gyo, or Heart
of Great Perfect Wisdom Sutra, follows the three prostrations. If you have a mokugyo, or hand drum, to chant
with, this can enhance the chanting practice.
When the sutra is finished, the chanting of
an eko, or dedication verse, is custom-
ary to transfer the merit of the
service to one's family, Buddhist
ancestors, or all beings in the
six realms. After the service
is completed, another set of
three prostrations brings the
practice to a close. This service
can be done any time of
the day in front of the
butsudan and is a great
way to follow one's
zazen practice daily.

40

The butsudan can also be used as a means to connect with your deceased family, friends, and teachers. Offering incense, candles, tea, or a treat that a loved one particularly enjoyed is a good way to remember those dear to us who have now departed.

The merits of a sutra recitation, or simply reading a Dharma book at the altar, can be done in the name of your loved ones as well, that the merit may find them wherever they are on their path to becoming buddhas. However one chooses to practice with the butsudan, the most important thing is that it serves as a focus for daily spiritual practice. The home altar is a place to make offerings, remember dear ones, and practice zazen and the Buddhadharma. It is not uncommon for the butsudan to be passed down from generation to generation within the family. Within the home altar you can find the three treasures of Buddha, Dharma, and Sangha.

Temple Altars

In Zen temples you will find an altar just about anywhere. This illustrates that the sacred is in all places. Throughout the temple complex you will find the sodo (monks' hall), the sanmon (gate), hatto (Dharma hall), Butsuden (Buddha hall), daikuin (kitchen), yokushitsu (bath), tosu (toilet), shidoden (memorial hall), kaisando (founders' hall), and kichijokaku (guest house) for housing visitors.

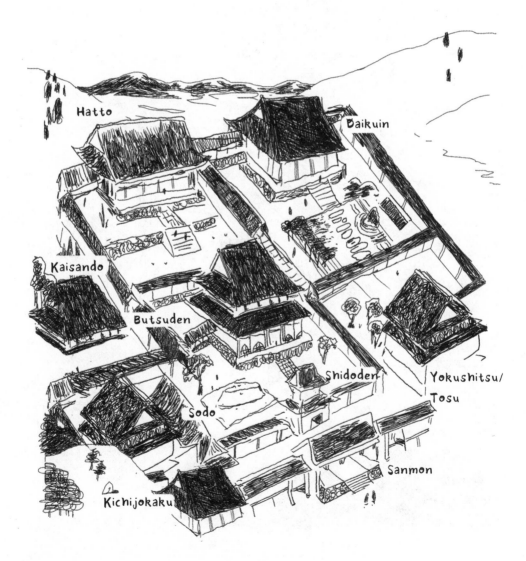

There is an altar for Ususama Myo-o in the lavatory where offerings, chanting, and bowing are done in front of the deity that protects the bathroom and burns up impurities. When using the bathroom at a Zen monastery, offering incense and reciting the gatha for using the bathroom are done at this altar to purify oneself and remove delusion.

In the kitchen you find Idaten standing in armor and holding a sword or club across his arms with hands in gassho. Offerings and chanting of the Heart of Great Perfect Wisdom Sutra and the Shosai Shu Dharani, the Removal of Disasters Dharani, are done at the kitchen altar, as Idaten is the protector of the kitchen and is associated with ample sustenance.

In the cemetery of the temple there are many images of Jizo Bodhisattva.
Jizo helps the deceased by traveling through the realms of existence and
saving sentient beings from suffering. Jizo is known as the protector of
children and travelers. A common altar for Jizo is called the roku Jizo, or
"six Jizo" altar representing Jizo's presence in each of the six realms. At a
Jizo altar, the typical offerings are flowers, incense, tea, food, and candles,
as well as two other offerings. Parents who've lost a child place children's
hats and bibs on the Jizo statues and toys on the altar.

The belief
is that Jizo
will find and
protect the
children in the
afterlife and
that these

offerings serve to alleviate the young
ones' suffering, until their karma is exhausted and they can be reborn in another
realm as they make their way to becoming
buddhas.

Of all the many altars in the Zen temple complex, the main one is in the hondo, or Dharma hall. This is where the main services are held. Morning service consists of chanting the Heart of Great Perfect Wisdom Sutra and offering the merit to Shakyamuni Buddha, Dogen Zenji, and Keizan Zenji. After this, the Sandokai, or Harmony of Difference and Equality, and the Hokyo Zanmai, or Precious Mirror Samadhi, are chanted for the benefit of the ancestral lineage, from the seven buddhas down to the founder of the temple in which the services are taking place.

The Dharma hall is the hall in which major services and holidays are held. The hondo altar typically has Shakyamuni Buddha at the center and may feature the bodhisattvas Fugen and Monju on either side. To the right of the altar you can see Dogen Zenji, and to the left is Keizan Zenji, the two founders of Soto Zen in Japan.

The kaisando is the founder's hall, which contains the relics of the founders, previous abbots, and teachers in the lineage of that particular temple. Portraits of the teachers and oihai, memorial tablets, dedicated to them are kept here. During the chanting of the Harmony of Relative and Absolute and the Precious Mirror Samadhi, the doshi will offer incense to these altars.

In the zendo, the most common altar you will see is one to Monju Bodhisattva. The reason is that Monju is the personification of the wisdom that comes from practicing the Buddhadharma. In the sodo, or monk's training hall, the Monju statue on the altar is called the Shoso Monju. The depiction of this bodhisattva differs from the traditional image because it shows a Monju depicted as an ordinary monk sitting zazen on a wild beast—a representation of the taming of the wild self through zazen.

Zazen
Sitting Zen

The zendo is the space for sitting zazen. There are manners for practicing in the zendo. Always keep your hands in shashu position when walking in the zendo. Bow in gassho toward the Buddha on the altar. This is a gesture of respect.

When moving about the zendo it is important not to run, jump, or walk with your hands at your sides. There should be no talking or horsing around in the zendo. Each sitting place will have a standard zazen setup. This consists of a round, pleated cushion filled with kapok or buckwheat hulls called a zafu. Under the zafu is the zabuton, a thick, flat cushion. If sitting on tatami mats, it is common to have a zafu without a zabuton underneath.

When you find a seat in the zendo, face the cushion
and bow in gassho. If there are people sitting in the spots
next to you, they will return the gesture.

Next, turn clockwise and bow in gassho again. Place your hands
on the platform and lift yourself up and back onto the zafu. Be
careful not to place your feet, legs, or bottom on the platform
as this is a sacred space. When you are settled on the zafu, spin
yourself around clockwise and face the wall.

Having settled on your zafu cushion, it is time to choose your posture. Cross your legs in either the full lotus, half lotus, or Burmese posture for zazen.

Full lotus position (kekka fuza):

Place the left foot on the right thigh and the right foot on the left thigh.

Half lotus position (hanka fuza):

Place the left foot on the right thigh, or the right on the left.

Burmese positon:

Place the left foot behind the right foot with the tops of the feet down.

If you are having difficulty sitting in the cross-legged position, or you are uncomfortable on a zafu, you can try these positions and seats as well.

The seiza bench is very popular for those who have a hard time crossing their legs. Seiza is a formal sitting position in Japan and is used when chanting sutras.

The wedge cushion is popular for those who sit in the Burmese position as it offers more height to fold the legs.

A chair may be a good solution for practitioners when other options don't work.

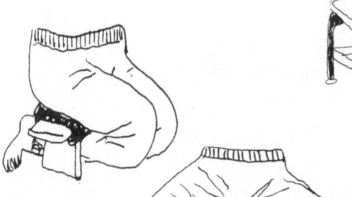

You should keep the bench under your sitting bones and adjust the height for comfort.

The wedge cushion has long edges to support your legs when in the Burmese posture.

Sit toward the front of the chair and do not lean against the back so that you can keep your spine straight.

54

This would be a really good time to discuss judgment when it comes to postures. There is a tendency to judge ourselves when we cannot sit in the posture that we desire. It can be damaging to our bodies to try to force a posture that is not possible for us to do. Over time, stretching and a regular zazen practice will loosen up our hips and joints so that we may be able to practice in our desired posture.

Additionally we shouldn't judge the postures of others. Thinking that full lotus on the zafu is the "right way" can lead to feeling superior or inferior to others. It is important to do your own zazen and not judge the practice of others. Self and others are not separate, so judging others has an effect on you. There is nothing wrong with sitting in a chair if you need to.

Haha, sitting in a chair.

Zazen is something that is done with body and mind. The two are actually not separate. When we hold an upright posture, the mind is bright and alert. When we slouch and bend at the spine, we lose our focus. The direct connection between our postures and our minds illustrates their unity. It is important to sit upright and keep the spine straight. The chin must be tucked in and the top of the head pointed up to the sky.

The lips and teeth are closed with the tongue on the roof of the mouth. Keeping the mouth closed and breathing through the nose is important, but don't close the mouth too tightly or you will develop a headache.

When you have found a posture that will work for you, place your hands, palms up, on top of your knees and begin to sway your body from left to right slowly. Gradually you should make each movement smaller and smaller, until you have found your center of gravity and are sitting up straight.

Next, place your arms gently at your sides and then rest your hands in your lap with the thumbs touching gently. Breathe in deeply through the nose and out through the mouth a few times. With your last exhalation, empty the lungs thoroughly so that your breathing becomes slow and natural. Begin breathing deeply and naturally.

The hands are held in the same position during zazen for any of the postures. Hand positions in Buddhism are called mudras. The mudra for zazen is called the hokkaijoin, or cosmic mudra. Place the right hand in the lap, palm facing upward, then place the left hand in the palm of the right facing up. The thumbs should touch lightly. You can gauge your state of mind based on the thumbs.

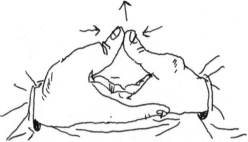

The thumbs pressing together tightly are an indicator that the mind is ruminating on thoughts. When you notice this, return your attention to your breathing and soften the pressure of your thumbs.

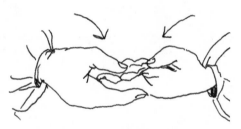

Thumbs not touching at all indicates that you are sleepy, daydreaming, or spaced out. Remember to bring your mind and your hands back to zazen.

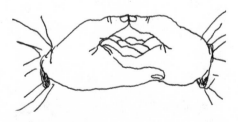

Thumbs gently touching in the hokkaijoin mudra for zazen.

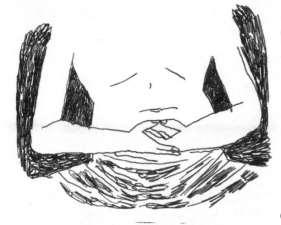

As you sit, it is important to keep the breath natural and full. This means not forcing your breath to be long or short. Simply let long breaths be long and short breaths be short. Breathe all the way down to your navel. This is the center of your body, called the tanden.

When you breathe out, your stomach should shrink inward. When you breathe in, your stomach should expand. Between breaths there is a quiet pause before the next breath; this is natural.

The type of zazen that is practiced in Soto Zen is called shikantaza, or just sitting. The point is not to do something unnatural or to attain some special state of mind that can be called "enlightenment." Soto Zen teaches that practice and enlightenment are not separate activities. To just sit in a quiet presence of one's life naturally is to express the nature of Buddha. This can be summed up by the teaching in Soto of Sokushinzebutsu, or "mind itself is Buddha."

Thoughts go in

Thoughts go out

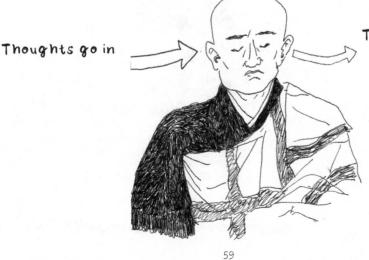

Susokukan: breath counting

Zazen with a koan

Zazen is not a means to an end or some goal. When the Buddha Shakyamuni attained enlightenment on December 8, after a week of long zazen practice, he continued to practice zazen all the way to the end of his life. Endless practice is the expression of the enlightened mind in Soto Zen Buddhism. Shikantaza is the "dropping off of body and mind," as Dogen Zenji proclaims. All goals, means to an end, and even the desire for enlightenment must drop away. While there are some forms of meditation in Zen Buddhism that relate to breath counting (called susokukan) or working with a teacher on a koan (that is, an historical case of an ancestor's awakening), these are not the same as the shikantaza practiced in Soto Zen.

Shikantaza

Endless practice

Doing meditation in steps toward enlightenment is not shikantaza. Through the practice of just sitting, we are able to continually let go of our delusions, goals, future, and past. By not holding on to anything, by just sitting, we are able to experience the truth of life, which is only experienced in the present moment, without adding anything to it that creates suffering. Clinging to ideals and pushing away unwanted experiences perpetuates our suffering. By just sitting we are able to "Let the true Dharma manifest," as written in the Fukanzazengi.

It is a common misconception that zazen is about not thinking, stopping thoughts, and having an empty mind. Unfortunately our brains store memories, opinions, preferences, desires, and conceptions. That is the brain's job. It works hard, and we cannot shut it off. If we did, we would be dead. People often say, "I just can't meditate. My thoughts keep getting in the way. I can't empty my mind."

You don't have to stop your thoughts. Zazen is about "opening the hand of thought," in the expression coined by Uchiyama Kosho Roshi. It means accepting everything as it is in the moment and not being separate from or attracted to anything.

The imaginary walls that we have built up throughout our lives that separate us from everything around us start to crack when we let our thoughts come and go without holding on to them. This is, in part, because no single thought can be identified as "me." All thoughts are just arisings, just temporary responses to causes and conditions. To understand the nature of "me," let's look at the example of a tomato.

Since childhood I have disliked the taste of raw tomatoes. I would eat foods that had cooked tomatoes in the ingredients, such as ketchup with fries, lasagna, pizza margarita, and even tomato soup. Yet never would I have put a tomato on my salad or sandwich because of the uncooked tomato flavor. My whole life I thought I was a person who just hated the taste of a raw tomato. Then I had a tomato on a caprese salad. I knew I hated raw tomatoes, but I did not want to be rude to my host, who had taken such pride in this offering of a beautiful caprese salad.

I took a bite,
chewed it up,
and swallowed it. I
loved it. This simple event blew my mind! Because of my preconceived notions about tomatoes, my not liking them, and my expectation that this preference would stay the same, I was able to see the Buddhist concept of anatman, or no-self.

For, if this self could change from hating to liking uncooked tomatoes in an instant, then that meant the self is always changing—that there is no fixed, permanent "me."

This is similar to what we see in zazen. Our thoughts come and go, and no permanent self can be found. The lines between inside, outside, us, and them start to seem less clear. Like clouds in the sky or waves in the ocean, thoughts come and go in our minds during zazen. We don't judge them as good or bad. We don't grab on to thoughts and elaborate on them, playing with them like toys. We just notice when we've picked them up, and then we set them down and come back to the unification of mind and body through the zazen posture.

We go through life trying to get things. Milk, money, success, fame, love, and sex. We have gaining minds, but zazen isn't done to gain anything—not to get enlightenment or even to become a better person. When done for those reasons, zazen ceases to be zazen and instead becomes a mode of self-improvement. Something to possess and make our lives more enjoyable. Zazen is the practice of waking up to the very present situation of our lives with a nonjudgmental mind, to be peacefully in the sea of Buddha nature.

This is not zazen, but a form of self-improvement:

Enlightenment

Hours spent in zazen

Following a period of zazen, there is kinhin. Kinhin is a form of walking zen. Kinhin is done with the same attitude as zazen. As you walk, let your thoughts come and go without holding on to them. When your mind wanders, come back to just walking.

With hands in gassho, bow forward at the sound of the bell.

For kinhin, when you hear two bells end a period of zazen, bow in gassho. Sway your body from left to right slowly, as you did when you started zazen. Take your time standing up from your seated position, as your legs may have fallen asleep during zazen. Brush off your zabuton and fluff the zafu into shape.

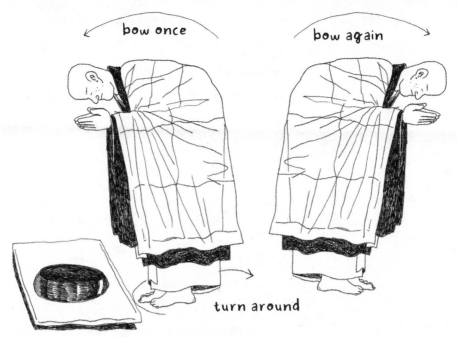

bow once

bow again

turn around

As before when you started zazen, bow in gassho toward your seat, then turn 180 degrees in gassho, and bow again away from your seat. Try to move in unison with the people next to you on either side, as you are practicing together in a spirit of harmony.

Place your hands in the shashu positon. This is done by placing your left thumb against your palm and wrapping your fingers around it in a fist.

Next, place your right hand in front of the left hand at the solar plexus with elbows now pointing outward on either side.

Finally, keep your eyes cast down at a 45-degree angle about three feet in front of you.

Turn to the left and begin walking in a clockwise direction around the zendo. Walk slowly, taking just half a step after one full in-and-out breath. The eyes are still at a 45-degree angle, not looking up or around the zendo. Keep walking in this way until you hear the kaishaku wooden clappers sound. Stop, then bow in gassho, and continue walking at a regular pace until you reach your seat in the zendo.

Upon returning to your seat, straighten your cushion, bow in gassho toward your seat, turn to the right clockwise, and bow in gassho away from your seat. Take the zazen posture and continue another period of zazen. This process will continue until the jikido (timekeeper) sounds a single bell to end the zazen period. When you hear the single bell, that signals that there will not be kinhin or another period of zazen. Stand up as before, place your hands in shashu, and exit the zendo.

Ceremony

There is a common misunderstanding about Zen Buddhism in relation to liturgical services and ceremony. Many people believe that real Zen has no religious services and that Zen's adherents do not consider Zen a religion. This may come from the stories about certain priests burning sutras, or Zen not relying on scripture, doctine, or dogma. The meaning of these stories is to convey nonattachment to one's idea of Buddha or enlightenment because this very attachment is delusion, in and of itself.

There is a famous story of the monk Tokusan Senkan (Deshan Xuanjian), who after having kensho, or an enlightening experience, brought all his commentaries on the Diamond Sutra to the front of the Buddha hall and said, "Even if you have exhausted abtruse doctrine, it is like placing a hair in vast space. Even if you have learned the vital points of all the truths in the world, it is like a drop of water thrown into a vast ravine." He then burned his commentaries on the sutra.

The truth is, Zen Buddhism has a rich history of ceremonies to mark major life events such as births, marriages, and deaths, and transfer of merit services. Taking the sixteen bodhisattva precepts is also an important ceremony to formalize one's commitment to practice the way of the Buddha. Every full moon, priests and practitioners come together to take refuge and renew their vows to follow the precepts in a ceremony called Fusatsu, or "renewal of vows." Ceremony is such a major part of Zen Buddhism that there are rituals for brushing one's teeth, using the toilet, bathing, and eating.

All of the mundane activities take on a spiritual significance when done with the heart of Zen practice. Part of what makes these activities significant is that we take the time to make ourselves aware of doing them. Chanting and

ceremony help to focus our attention on activities. Another reason to chant the sutras is to express our gratitude to the buddhas and ancestors for their teaching. We offer the merit of the recitation of these sutras to all sentient beings that they may realize an end to their suffering. Before and after recitation of the sutras, we do prostrations to bow in gratitude and respect to Buddha and the awakened mind.

There are many people who want to sit zazen and have a great aversion to ceremony. Their main focus is zazen, and ceremony is looked at as something that can be thrown out. This tends to be a problem for many, as this can lead to practicing zazen as a means of bettering oneself. This turns zazen into a selfish activity. Getting up off the zafu and chanting sutras makes the body, speech, and mind expressions of enlightened activity. Chanting is also another form of moving zazen.

73

There are many activities to follow in ceremonies: cues to bow, mudras to hold your hands in, the offering of merit to all sentient beings and movements in harmony with the other practitioners. This is no different from zazen. When practicing ceremony in this way, there is no difference between zazen and brushing the teeth, using the toilet, chanting sutras, or walking kinhin. When practicing Zen it is important not only to take the parts you like, but not to discard the parts you don't like. Trust the practice that has been handed down from the buddhas and ancestors to this very day, and have faith in your ability to realize the Dharma.

If we take only the parts we like about Zen, then we are just building up a big, new deluded self. It is important to sit zazen even if one doesn't feel like it or to chant sutras even if one doesn't feel like it. Whether you like or dislike practice is irrelevant. Give up picking and choosing and you are as free as the vast sky. The sutras that are most often chanted during the day in the temple are:

Kanzeon Bosatsu Fumonbonge
The Kanzeon Chapter of the Lotus Sutra

This sutra is a chapter from the Lotus Sutra that describes the aspects of Kanzeon Bodhisattva. Kanzeon is the bodhisattva that responds to the suffering of all beings. The sutra states that all one needs to do in a time of need is to call wholeheartedly on this bodhisattva and the suffering will be alleviated. As the sutra states, "When living beings suffer hardships, burdened by immeasurable woes, the power of Kanzeon's wondrous wisdom can relieve the suffering of the world."

Sandokai and Hokyo Zanmai

Harmony of Relative and Absolute and the Jewel Mirror Samadhi

These sutras are chanted together in honor of the ancestral teachers. The two sutras are dedicated to the ancestral line from Shakyamuni Buddha down to the most recent deceased ancestor in one's Dharma lineage.

Maka Hanya Haramita Shin Gyo
Maha Prajna Paramita Heart Sutra

This sutra is the distillation of the Buddhist teaching on emptiness. The sutra states that all phenomena experienced through the five skandhas of form, feeling, volition, perception, and consciousness are empty of any permanent, individual self. All things that arise are dependent upon causes and conditions and are empty of any enduring nature. A famous line from the sutra states that form is emptiness and emptiness is form; the same is also true of all sensation, thought, activity, and consciousness. The sutra finishes with the introduction of the mantra *Gate gate, paragate, parasam gate, bodhi svaha*, meaning "Gone, gone, gone beyond, the other shore, rejoice!"

Fukanzazengi
Universal Recommendation for Zazen

Fukanzazengi was written by Eihei Dogen Zenji, composed after Dogen had returned to Japan from his training with Tendo Nyojo in China. In this work Dogen discusses steps to be taken when practicing zazen, the mind during zazen, and how to arise from sitting zazen. In Soto Zen temples and monasteries throughout the world the Fukanzazengi is chanted daily by the sangha. It has been often overlooked by some as being only an introduction to zazen, but the Fukanzazengi has a wealth of teaching on Soto Zen philosophy in the text. "The way is originally perfect and all-pervading. What need is there for practice and realization?" Dogen makes clear that there is no separation between practice and enlightenment. Later Dogen states, "Now, if you make the slightest discrimination, you will create a gap like that between heaven and earth." This further illustrates the importance of the understanding of Dogen's practice-enlightenment.

Daihi Shin Dharani

Great Compassionate Mind Dharani

The Daihi Shin Dharani is one of the most popular chants in Soto Zen Buddhism. The dharani is in adoration to Kanzeon, bodhisattva of great compassion. This dharani is used to generate great compassion within the chanter as well as to generate compassion within the world for the benefit of all sentient beings. The importance of the dharani is not necessarily in the meaning of the words, but in the act of chanting the sounds of the dharani. This is why the dharani is not typically translated for chanting. The Daihi Shin Dharani is a list of the attributes of the Bodhisatva Kanzeon and describes the actions of the compassionate mind. As with all texts, to further understand all sides of this multidimensional work, studying a translation is important.

Kanromon

Ambrosia Gate

The Kanromon is chanted for the gaki
(hungry ghosts) and spirits of those who have
no ancestors to remember them or transfer merit on their behalf. Kanromon serves to feed the gaki as well as transfer merit for them, that they
may be able to find their way out of the hungry ghost realm. The dharani
that are part of this chant are:

Dharani for Inviting the Cloudlike Hosts of Spirits

Dharani for Breaking Down the Gates of Hell and Opening Throats

Dharani for Sanctifying Food with Innumerable Virtues

Dharani for Bestowing the Ambrosial Taste

Dharani for Contemplating Vairocana Buddha

Dharani for Invoking the Five Tathagatas

Dharani for Producing the Thought of Enlightenment

Dharani for Giving the Bodhisattva Precepts

Dharani for Dwelling in the Jeweled Pavilion

Dharani for Initiation into the Radiance of Buddhas

The eko, or verse for generating merit, that
follows these dharanis illustrates the importance of this ceremony:

"With the good karma gathered in this
practice, we repay the virtuous toils of our
fathers and mothers, that the living may
be blessed with joy and long life without
distress, and the deceased freed from suffering. May the four benefactors, sentient
beings in the three classes of existence, and
those born in three evil destinies and eight
difficulties all be able to repent their
transgressions, purify their intent,
and entirely escape the round of
rebirth, and be born in the Pure Land."

Clothing and Vestments

The many cultures that Buddhism has moved through have left an imprint on the clothing worn by its monks and priests. From Buddhism's origins in India, monks wore the kasaya, or o-kesa. Under the o-kesa is the koromo, which has its origins in China. Originally the koromo was worn as a two-piece garment in India, but it was sewn together in China where the climate was much colder. The large sleeves on the koromo are due to the style of Chinese garments of the time. Under the koromo are the kimono and juban, the traditional Japanese garments. Each piece of clothing has a traditional style for wearing, folding, and storing, as they should be treated with respect and care. These items represent the three jewels of Buddha, Dharma, and Sangha, as well as one's bodhisattva vows, as is the case with the o-kesa and rakusu.

Chinese robes

Japanese robes

Theravada robes (Southeast Asia)

Korean robes

Shukin

The shukin is a cord belt that is worn around the waist of a priest when wearing a koromo. Shukin help keep the posture straight during zazen as they are tied around the upper abdomen and keep you from slumping over. If one were to slouch, the shukin would become uncomfortable. The shukin also keeps the collars of the juban, kimono, and koromo neat and uniform as they do not move around when they are tied under the shukin. Below are the steps to tie the shukin.

The shukin untied

Wrap the shukin around your waist like a belt and tie it in a bow in front.

Take two of the six loops. Place the other four loops through them, two on each side. Next, pull the two loops tight.

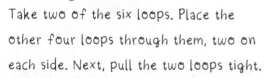

Wrap the four leftover loops around the shukin belt, like so, and then pull them tight.

The shukin in its final tied state

To put the shukin away:

Take the shukin and loop it around
twice, then place your hands through it.

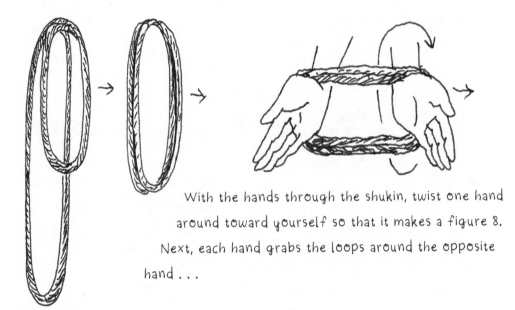

With the hands through the shukin, twist one hand
around toward yourself so that it makes a figure 8.
Next, each hand grabs the loops around the opposite
hand . . .

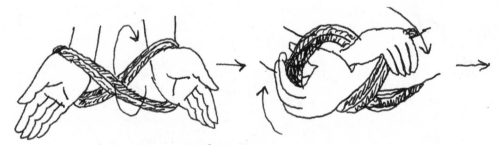

. . . and tightly pulls each loop of the shukin.

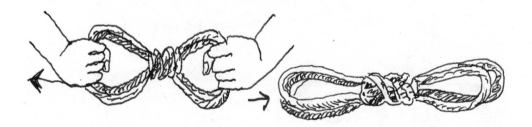

Now the shukin is ready to be put away until the next use.

Kimono

The kimono is worn underneath the koromo. For priests, the color of the kimono should be subdued and without a pattern— gray, blue, brown, and the like. A more formal version of the kimono is called a hakue, and it is used for ceremonies, especially during ordination. This garment is white and has the same shape as the kimono. Underneath the kimono or hakue is the juban, a traditional Japanese under- shirt. The collar of the juban should show a little from under the kimono. The ki- mono should not be too short and should fall to the ankle. The collar of the kimono is closed left over right and should not be too loose around the neck, lest it come open or become messy when moving. It is all right to hang the kimono up, but there is a special way to fold the kimono for traveling or for storing the kimono when not in use. The steps for folding are as follows.

Lay the kimono out flat on the floor and then fold the right front side over to the middle of the garment while keeping the sleeve flat out on the floor, as pictured below. Do this again with the left side as well, so that it is matching the right.

Next, fold the kimono, from the bottom, up until the hem comes up to the middle.

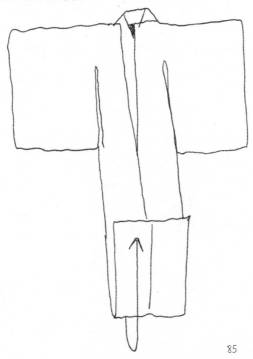

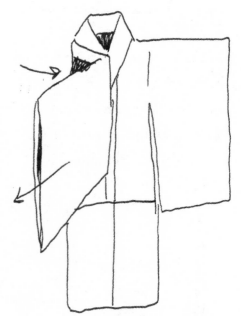

Fold the right sleeve inward at the shoulder in an accordian fold.

Take the left sleeve and fold it in the same fashion, accordian style to the right.

At this point, with the sleeves folded in, the kimono is still lying flat on its back with the hem folded up to the middle.

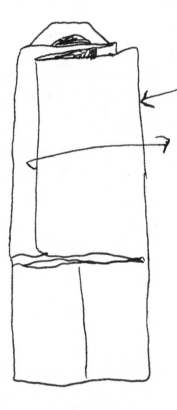

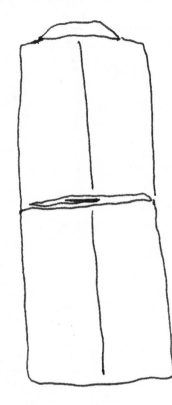

Fold the kimono again from the bottom upwards to the collar. At this point brush out any wrinkles and crease the edges with your fingers.

Place the kimono in the center of a large square of fabric called a furoshiki, and fold the edges around each side for storage.

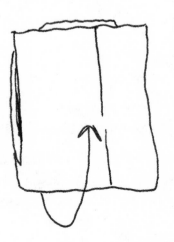

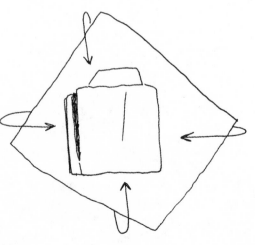

Rakusu

The rakusu is an abbreviated form of the o-kesa and is worn by priests in informal settings. The rakusu is also worn by Zen Buddhists who have taken the sixteen bodhisattva precepts in a ceremony called Jukai. When handling the rakusu, it is important to treat it with respect. This means that you should not leave it lying around on the floor, wrinkle it up, or stack things on top of it. Instead, you should fold the rakusu, keep it in a cloth or case, keep it clean, and take it off when eating food so as not to stain it.

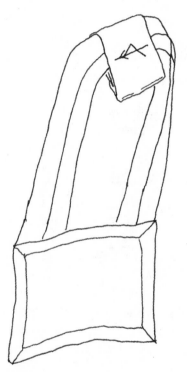

The rakusu may be sewn by a practitioner or purchased through a Dharma group when one has been given permission to participate in the Jukai service. Before a Jukai service, a priest will write the name of the temple, practice center, or group as well as the date the precepts were given to the practitioner. The new Dharma name will be written on the back of the rakusu as well. This name is decided by the teacher to be a description of the practitioner's character, as well as an aspirational attribute of one's Dharma practice. The priest then signs the rakusu to certify that the precepts were given to the practitioner, and a lineage chart called the kechimyaku, or bloodline of the buddhas, is given along with the precepts. This is a chart that shows the line of the precepts being passed from Shakyamuni Buddha down to the Buddhist who is receiving them now. The line then continues back to before Shakyamuni Buddha, showing the continuous chain of the precepts. Buddha gives them to Buddha.

There is a specific way one should take off the rakusu. Again, these forms are a part of Zen practice and are adhered to as a way to express respect and devotion to Buddha, Dharma, and Sangha. First, with your right hand reach under the rakusu neck straps, and with your left hand take the bottom corners of the front and pinch them together. This will fold the rakusu in half as you lift the straps over your head.

Next, straighten out the straps of the rakusu and keep the body folded in half. Make sure that you are folding it neatly. The straps should be accordian-folded down, and then up. Keep the stitching of the Soto pine symbol facing up.

Finally, fold the rakusu in half again. Make sure that when you fold the rakusu, you keep your teacher's name and signature facing up, as this shows respect for the teacher who gave you the precepts.

O-kesa

The o-kesa is worn by the "home leaver," or priest, in Soto Zen Buddhism. There are different colors of o-kesa that represent the different ranks of priests. Novices wear a black o-kesa until they have attained the status of osho, or teacher. Then they wear a more traditional brown or orange robe that is seen in other schools of Buddhism. Very senior priests, or dai-osho, can be seen wearing a deep purple, red, or even brocade o-kesas. Since Shakyamuni Buddha's time, only ordained monks or priests wear the o-kesa, a robe traditionally sewn together from discarded scraps of fabric that have

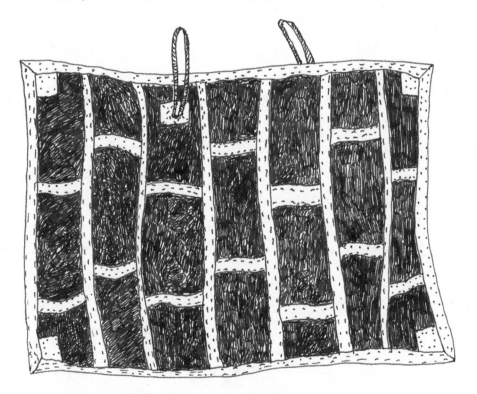

been washed and dyed to a mustard color. The panels are sewn in a pattern that represents a rice field. This is explained in a story in which Buddha is asked by the monk Ananda, his attendant, what the robes of a priest should look like. As Buddha looks out at farmers working in a rice field, he marvels at the beauty and informs Ananda to make the robes patchwork, like a rice field. The o-kesa represents the very teachings of Buddha and is worn during ceremonies, chanting, and zazen.

Practicing with the o-kesa is a way that we connect to our Dharma lineage in the past, present, and future. The ceremony for the o-kesa has been handed down from generation to generation and is brought to us by the founder of Soto Zen in Japan, Eihei Dogen Zenji. The ceremony takes place after morning zazen, and the Kesa Verse is recited in unison by the community. The clappers strike once, and everyone in the zendo puts their hands in gassho and chants three times:

"Great robe of liberation, a formless field of merit. Wrapping ourselves in Buddha's teaching, we free all living beings."

Each member of the sangha then puts on their o-kesa, or rakusu, and continues zazen until the final bell strike indicating the end of zazen. This ceremony takes place only after morning zazen. For the remainder of the day zazen can be done wearing the o-kesa, or rakusu.

When not being worn, the o-kesa should be folded neatly, placed in a cloth case, and stored in a respectful place. It is not appropriate to keep the o-kesa on the floor or in a clothing drawer. The o-kesa can be kept by the altar or on the zafu at one's zazen spot. Always care for the o-kesa in a respectful way, keeping it clean and unwrinkled. It is common to store the o-kesa with a pouch of powdered incense to keep it pure, as incense symbolizes burning away impurities, healing, and making an offering to the three treasures of Buddha, Dharma, and Sangha. The o-kesa represents the Buddha, Dharma, and Sangha.

Zagu

Prostration Cloth

The zagu is a prostration cloth that is carried by Zen priests whenever they are wearing their o-kesa. It is a long cloth the same color as the priest's o-kesa, folded in on itself vertically and draped over the left arm, under the koromo. The priest uses the zagu when doing prostrations, during service, and to sit down on while chanting sutras. The origins of the zagu go back to India when priests would sit zazen on the ground. The zagu was a mat, typically straw, that would be placed under the meditation seat of the monk. The zagu keeps the the robe clean while the monk sits zazen, sleeps, and takes meals. Today, the zagu is used as a ceremonial prostration cloth and is rarely used to sit outdoors directly on the ground.

Folding and storing the zagu:

Opened zagu   Accordian fold inward   Fully folded zagu

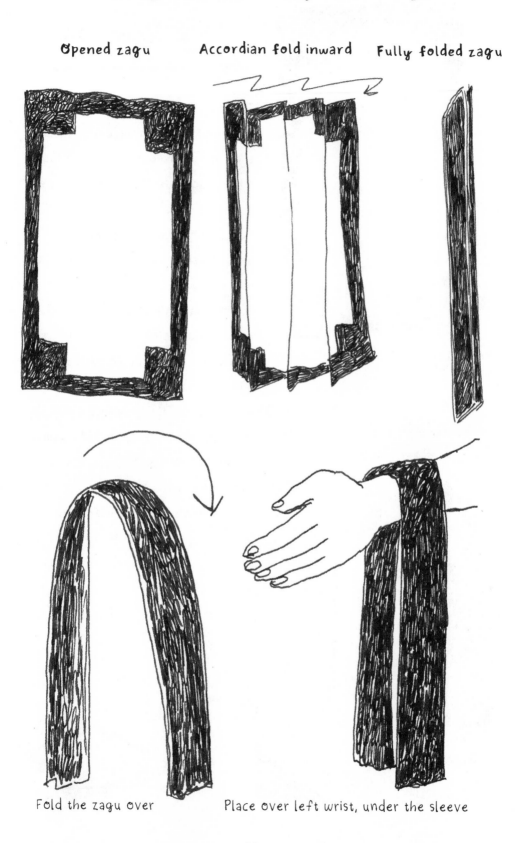

Fold the zagu over   Place over left wrist, under the sleeve

Koromo

The koromo is a long-sleeved robe of Chinese origin. The original Buddhist garments in India were a two-piece top and bottom that covered the torso and legs. But because the Chinese climate is much colder, the robe transformed into a more traditional Chinese garment. The top and bottom were sewn together and combined with the long sleeves of Chinese robes. When sitting zazen, the sleeves of the koromo are folded on top of the heels, under the hands, and act as a rest for the zazen mudra.

The koromo is traditionally black, but depending on the rank of one's status as a priest, it can be seen in different colors. A yellow koromo may be worn for only the highest position. For an abbot, jōkeshi, or godo (head of a training hall), a red koromo can be worn. Black is worn by the osho (temple priest). For the kyoshi rank priest (priest who can ordain and train priests) a blue, gray, or black robe may be worn. The unsui (cloud-water monk) wears only black.

The koromo should be cared for with respect. It should not be worn in the bathroom and should be hung up or folded when not being worn. Follow these steps when removing the koromo.

Step 1

Put the koromo on backward and reach down to the bottom corners of the sleeves. Put your pointer fingertips into the sleeves and stretch out your arms. Put the ends of your sleeves together, take out one hand and hold the sleeves out to the side.

Step 2

Holding the sleeves out to the side, fold the garment in half by bringing the ends of the sleeves to the opposite corner below the chin.

Step 3

Fold the koromo in half by dropping the collar down over both arms as shown to the left. Make sure to keep the fabric neat and free of wrinkles by folding with great attention to the movement of the hands and pleats of the garment.

Step 4

Finally, fold the koromo in half again to complete the process.

Now you have a neatly folded koromo to wrap in a furoshiki.

Samue

Samue are work clothes worn by priests and lay practitioners alike. They are extra comfortable! Samue can be worn during samu, chanting, or informal zazen. Samue can be worn with a T-shirt or dressed up with a juban underneath. Samue are loose-fitting and can be worn during zazen as well.

Samue should be blue, black, brown, or gray as these subdued colors are not distracting in the Zen center.

Major Holidays

In Zen, there are many different ceremonies and events that take place throughout the year. These practice days and religious observances commemorate our past family ancestors, monks, and teachers, as well as important dates in the liturgical calendar. Let's take a look at some of the most significant of these.

Obon

Obon is one of the most important holidays in Buddhism. The summer festival of Obon honors the spirits of deceased ancestors. It is a time to make offerings to family members, friends, and even pets who've passed away, as well as to spirits who have no one left to honor and remember them. These spirits are called hungry ghosts. A chant named Kanromon is chanted; offerings of rice, water, and vegetables are placed on the altar. All the doors and windows of the temple are opened so that the spirits can enter, eat, and return back to their place in the six realms, having been sustained by the offerings. The merit of the chanting and offerings made to the buddhas and bodhisattvas is transferred to these spirits that they may find their way to buddhahood.

The term *Obon* is the shortened version of Urabon-e, or Ullambana, a Sanskrit word meaning "to hang upside down." Because the suffering in the realm of hungry ghosts is like the pain of hanging upside down, this ceremony is called Ullabana. The story of Obon says that when Mokuren, or Maudgalyayana in Sanskrit, a disciple of the Buddha, was sitting in meditation, he saw a vision of his deceased mother as a hungry ghost wandering in search of food. When she was able to find some and tried to eat it, it turned to fire in her mouth before she could swallow it. When she found water, it turned to pus. Maudgalyayana told Buddha of this vision, saying how tormented he was by his mother's suffering.

The Buddha then instructed Maudgalyayana to make offerings to the other monks in the sangha and transfer the merit to his suffering mother. Maudgalyayana did this, and then later he had a vision that his mother's karma had been exhausted, and her time in the realm of hungry ghosts had ended. Maudgalyayana was so happy that he began to dance. This is where the tradition of dancing the Bon Odori, or Bon dance, which happens at the end of Obon, originated.

During Obon,
family offers
the deceased's
favorite food
and drink on
the altar.

Many different types of sweets and cakes are offered to the gaki who
wander in. Lanterns are lit outside of one's home or temple and the doors
are opened to welcome the spirits of the departed to come home to eat,
drink, and dance. When the ceremony is over, the lanterns are floated on a
river that is close to one's home or temple to bring the spirits back out of
this human realm and into the realm they came from.

Rohatsu Sesshin and Jodo-e

Rohatsu Sesshin is observed from December 1 through 8. This sesshin is the most intense zazen practice of the year because its purpose is to commemorate the enlightenment of Shakyamuni Buddha. For seven days, practitioners sit zazen, only taking breaks for meals—which take place in the zendo oryoki-style—for kinhin, samu, chanting, and sleep. Some Zen temples even encourage practitioners to sleep while sitting up in the zazen posture all through the night of December 7. The end of Rohatsu marks the celebration of Jodo-e, the day that the Buddha attained enlightenment upon seeing the morning star after sitting deep in zazen. On the morning of December 8, incense is lit; offerings of candles, flowers, fruit, sweet water, tea, and sweets are offered on the altar; and sutras are chanted. The merit of these offerings is given to Shakyamuni Buddha out of gratitude for the Dharma.

Hanamatsuri

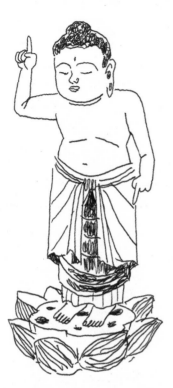

April 8 is the celebration of Shakyamuni Buddha's birth. It is called Hana Matsuri, or Flower Festival. The ceremony consists of setting up an altar representing Lumbini Garden, the birthplace of the Buddha. The altar is covered with flowers and a statue of the baby Buddha pointing upward to heaven and downward to earth is placed in a basin of tea. Adherents offer powdered incense and then ladle the tea over the baby Buddha in a gesture that represents bathing the newborn. Later, tea is given to the temple-goers.

The baby Buddha is pointing to heaven above and earth below, showing that he is the World-Honored One.

Ohigan

Ohigan means "the other shore," or the shore of nirvana. This service takes place twice a year during the spring and fall equinoxes, and it is a time to visit family graves and offer incense, candles, flowers, and food. Family members clean the grave sites in reverence for their relatives and friends who've passed away. They recite sutras and offer prayers for their loved ones, reminding themselves of the preciousness of life and expressing their gratitude.

Offering incense, candles, flowers, tea, and fruit to the buddhas and bodhisattvas is also common during this time. Ohigan is a time to clean and reorganize the butsudan, or home altar, and also to sit zazen. During Ohigan the emphasis is on the study of what it means to practice on this shore as a bodhisattva.

Nehan-e

Nehan-e is the ceremony commemorating the death of Shakyamuni Buddha, who passed away in Kushinagara between sala trees that are said to have burst into bloom out of season at the time of his passing.

Practitioners chant sutras and pay homage to the Buddha with offerings of sweets, candles, flowers, tea, and incense. During the service, the celebrants scatter paper lotus-flower petals around the altar as they ambulate around the Buddha hall and recite dharani, a type of powerful petitionary prayer, and the chapter "The Lifespan of the Tathagata" of the Lotus Sutra. After the service, adherents collect the paper lotus petals and bring them home.

Shotsuki Memorial Service

Memorials take place throughout the year to commemorate people's passing. Priests offer food, tea or coffee, incense, candles, flowers, fruit, and the recitation of the Daihishin Dharani, or Great Compassionate Mind Dharani. Even when the death of a loved one happened decades earlier, families still show up on the anniversary of that person's death to bring flowers and food for the offerings and, in turn, to offer incense and chanting. Because of this, Shotsuki memorials are very moving services.

Many temples keep a record of sangha members who have passed away, bring out the oihai memorial tablets during the month of their passing, and offer this same memorial service. The dedication, practice, and commitment to building a sangha by the late members' generosity is repaid by the offering of merit, food, drink, and sutras.

Sesshin

Sesshin take place throughout the year and are a chance to collect the mind and rest within the silent space of zazen. Generally, sesshin last for seven days, but they can be as short as three days. Single-day sittings are called zazenkai, and they follow a similar structure of zazen, chanting, and oryoki as that of sesshin.

These are the most common events and holidays we observe in Soto Zen Buddhism, but each temple and center may have their own traditions that they follow on the calendar as well.

Narashimono: Instruments

Densho

The densho is the main hall bell. It indicates when the hall is ready for a ceremony and when the ceremony will begin. The ringing of the densho has three rounds with seven, five, and then three strikes. Each round is followed by a roll-down—a series of strikes that become closer and closer together.

The first round of the densho tells the community that the incense, candles, charcoal, and flowers are ready on the altar. The second round indicates that the ryoban, or participating community, is entering the hall. The third round signals that the doshi, or officiant of the service, is ready to enter the hall.

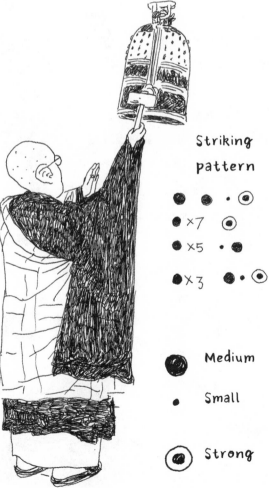

Striking pattern

● ● · ◉
● ×7 ◉
● ×5 · ●
● ×3 ●·◉

● Medium

· Small

◉ Strong

Keisu Bell

A keisu is a bowl-shaped bell that rests on a cushion. The special striker used to hit the keisu bell is called the bai. Large keisu are used for chanting services to indicate incense offerings, sutra titles, and eko (dedication of merit from sutra recitations).

Small keisu are used to mark the moments when the sangha should sit down or stand up during the service, or when the sutra, mantra, or dharani is coming to an end during chanting. Keisu are also used to signal the beginning and end of zazen.

The bai is used to hit the edge of the keisu in a forward motion to produce the long ring of the bell. When the bell is to be silenced for the chant titles, the bai is hit against the edge of the keisu and then held in place. This technique is called a gats.

Bai

Keisu

Moppan

The great matter is birth and death. Life passes swiftly and time is gone. Wake up! Don't waste time.

The moppan is a wooden plaque that is struck with a wooden mallet to indicate that zazen is to commence. On its surface you will often find inscribed some variation of the verse: "The great matter is birth and death. Life passes swiftly and time is gone. Wake up! Don't waste time." As with the densho, each round on the moppan follows the seven-, five-, and three-round pattern, and each round is concluded with a ring-down.

The practitioner to the right is striking a round on the moppan to indicate that all the community should enter the zendo to begin a period of zazen. After the third round on the moppan, zazen will commence and those who are late will not be permitted into the zendo until kinhin, or an appropriate time.

Mokugyo

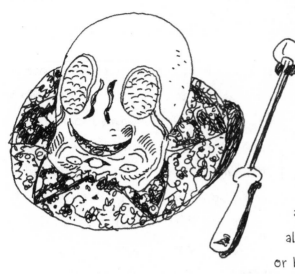

The mokugyo is a wooden drum carved into the shape of two fish face to face. The reason for this comes from the belief that fish always have their eyes open, so they are always awake. Practitioners should always strive to "wake up," or become enlightened. The mokugyo is used to keep the rhythm of the sutra chanting. The drum is struck with a soft mallet by the doan. Another wooden fish drum called the gyoku is used to announce the beginning of meals in the dining hall.

The gyoku hanging from the ceiling outside the dining hall. The gyoku may also be found hanging outside the zendo by the gaitan, as in Zen monasteries the meals are eaten in the sodo, or zendo.

Inkin

The inkin is a handheld bell used to lead the doshi in a procession or recession. It also alerts participants in the chanting service to do prostrations. The inkin can also be used to mark periods of zazen or in place of a keisu, if one is not available.

The inkin may have a silk or brocade cloth covering the handle.

An alternate form of an inkin has a small mokugyo attached to the side. This can be used in services or in a particular place, such as at a gravesite, in a sangha member's home, or while chanting in a circumambulation.

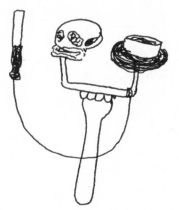

Oryoki: Meditative Eating

The history of oryoki—the formal practice of taking a meal—goes back
to the time of Shakyamuni Buddha, over 2,500 years ago. In those days,
monks wandered the Indian subcontinent between practice periods (ango)
and carried nothing but a robe and a bowl. They would beg in villages
for their meals, and donors would put food in their bowls—just enough
for the monks to sustain themselves. The monks would move on after
the ango period so as not to be too much of a strain on the villagers with
regard to receiving meals.

While the practice of begging for food, or alms, is still practiced to this day, there was a big shift in how monks received their food when Buddhism spread to China. Monks began to grow their own food and work the land to harvest crops. In addition to this transformation, there were also changes to the way monks ate their meals. More bowls were added, more ceremony, but the same spirit of mindful eating, gratitude, and interdependence remained. *Oryoki* means "vessel that contains just enough," and it refers not just to the food bowls but to the entire meal practice: serving and receiving the food, eating, cleaning the dishes, and putting them away. Food is like medicine—it supports our health and well-being so that we can practice the Buddhadharma.

Dogen states in his work Tenzo Kyokun, or Instructions to the Chief Cook, that a cook should not consider the quality of ingredients, whether expensive or cheap, and should treat them as equal because they are precious.

In the same way, practitioners should not consider the flavor of the food that's being offered to them.

During an oryoki meal you eat what is offered, regardless of preference of flavors.

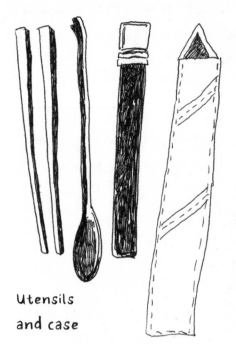

Utensils and case

Let's take a look at what an oryoki set contains. The utensil set includes chopsticks, a spoon, and a setsu. A setsu is a type of spatula that is used to clean the bowls. Next there is a wrapping cloth, lap cloth, and wiping cloth. There is a set of five bowls. Bowl one is the Buddha bowl and stacked inside it are bowls two, three, four, and five. Bowl one always contains the grain of the meal such as rice, oatmeal, and porridge. Bowl two holds a soup dish, or the secondary vegetarian dish. The third bowl contains pickles or seasonings. Bowls four and five typically are stacked under bowl three, unless other food offerings are available.

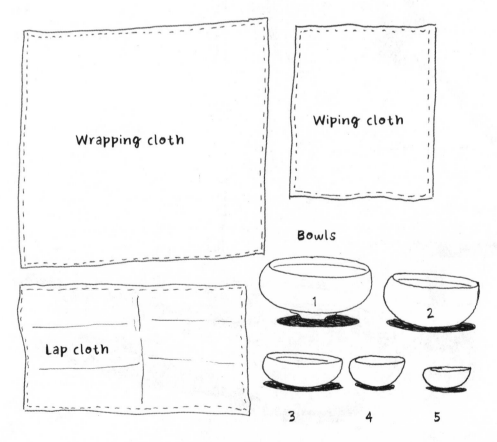

Wrapping cloth

Wiping cloth

Lap cloth

Bowls

1

2

3 4 5

There are particular ways to handle the oryoki. When walking with oryoki, always keep it at eye level. Do not store the oryoki on the floor or underneath furniture. Always carry the oryoki set with two hands. Always

keep oryoki sets in a high place, like a shelf, out of respect. In many temples there is a shelf in the zendo that is for the oryoki.

Also make sure to carry the oryoki set in a specific way. Always keep the pinky fingers and thumbs touching. There are particular ways to handle the Buddha bowl.

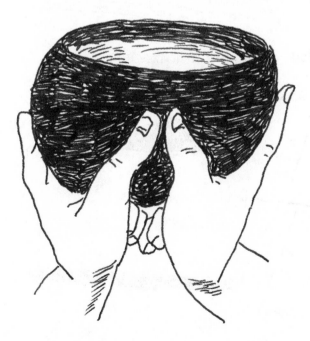

This bowl represents the Buddha, so you want to make sure you handle it with respect. Don't ever touch the Buddha bowl to your lips when you are eating. It is all right to do so with the other bowls.

Let's look at how to set up your oryoki set for a meal. When you hear the kaishaku wooden clappers strike, bow in gassho with the oryoki in front of you. First you untie the oryoki set as follows:

Untie the knot and spread the cloth.

Remove the wiping cloth and utensil bag.

Rotate and place them in front of you.

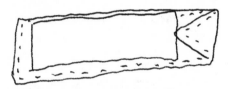

Take the corners of the lap cloth, pull it open, and place it in your lap.

Open all the edges of the wrapping cloth and
spread them out into a diamond shape.

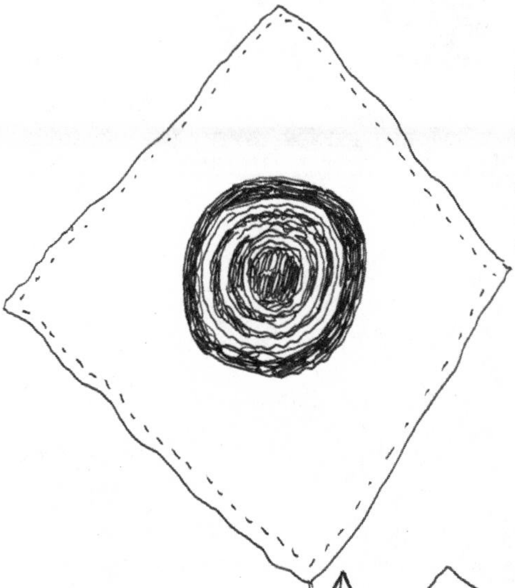

Next, fold each of the ends in an
accordian-style inward, then outward,
so that your place setting looks as
shown to the left. Slide the stacked
bowls over to the left of the setting.

Using your index finger,
push the two smallest bowls
on top out and place them to
the right of the place setting.

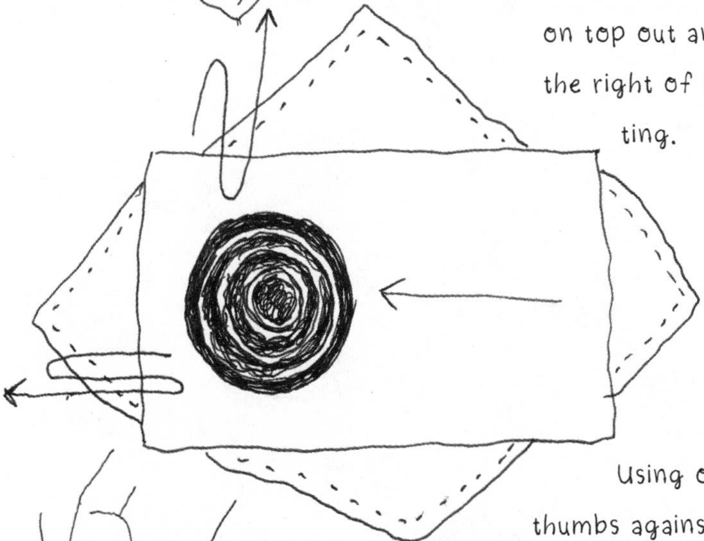

Using only your
thumbs against the inside of
the bowls, move them over to
the right, with the smallest bowl
first, then the larger bowl in
the center.

Your setting should now look like this, with the Buddha bowl on your left followed by the smaller bowls to the right.

Take the utensil case and take out the chopsticks first. Next, take out the spoon.

And finally the setsu should be taken out and flipped so that the cloth side is facing down.

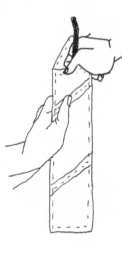
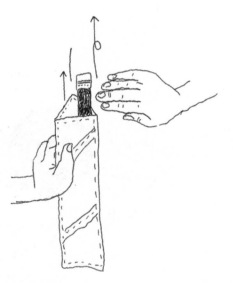

This set is ready for food to be served.

At this point in the meal, the servers will approach in between two trainees and bow. At the same time the two trainees will bow and then be served.

Bowing

Bowing

Hold out your bowl and the server will place food in it. When you have received enough food, you raise your hand slightly, palm upward. Only then will the server stop putting food in your bowl.

After you and your neighbor have been served, you bow in unison.

At the appropriate time in the meal chant, place your spoon in the Buddha bowl with the handle facing away from you.

Place the chopsticks over the middle bowl with the handles facing in the eleven o'clock position. Raise up the Buddha bowl with both hands and bring it to eye level for the following verse: "May we all realize the Buddha Way."

Before putting the Buddha bowl back down in its place, take three small bites of the rice or oats dish. These are for the three treasures, four benefactors, and beings in the six realms. At this point it is all right to put the Buddha bowl down and put the seasonings from the third bowl in the Buddha bowl if there are any. When eating your meal, it is very important to know that only the spoon is used in the Buddha bowl and not the chopsticks. The chopsticks are for the other dishes. Do not use the spoon for another bowl even if you are eating soup. Use the chopsticks for the soup and drink from the bowl.

When the meal has ended, use the setsu to clean up and eat any food particles that are left in each bowl.

When everyone is finished, the kaishaku will clap, and the servers will come around with hot water or tea.

Bow, as before, and hold up your bowl. The server will then pour in the liquid.

Again, raise your hand palm up when you have enough.

Use the setsu to clean the Buddha bowl and then pour the liquid into the next bowl. Dry the Buddha bowl and then place it back in its place with the drying cloth still in the bowl. Next, wash the utensils in the middle bowl and put them away. Continue washing and pouring the liquid into the bowls until you reach the last one.

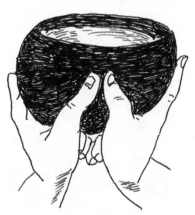

Place all the bowls back into the Buddha bowl and slide the bowls back to the middle of the wrapping cloth. Pull the edges of the cloth out flat.

Take the top and bottom ends and fold them over the bowls.

Take the lap cloth and fold it back up and place it on top of the oryoki.

Take the utensil case and wiping cloth and place them on top of the oryoki set.

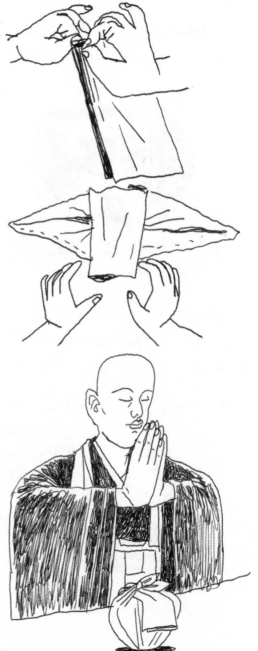

And finally wrap the oryoki back up as it was in the beginning. Gassho and bow. Now the meal is finished. Take the oryoki set and bring it back to where it is stored in its respected place.

Jukai: The Bodhisattva Precepts

In the Soto Zen tradition, practitioners follow a road map to reduce the suffering of all beings. This road map is comprised of sixteen precepts called the bodhisattva precepts, which guide us along through life. Thinking of the precepts as a guide rather than as a set of rules imposed on us is an accurate way to describe them. They are something alive, and we can work with them in our lives. The buddhas and bodhisattvas point the way out of suffering through the precepts.

The precepts start with the three refuges. By taking refuge in the three treasures of Buddha, Dharma, and Sangha, we can begin to work with the precepts. Taking refuge in the Buddha is taking refuge in the mind of awakening.

By taking refuge in the Dharma, we are taking refuge in the teachings of Buddha. We can look around us in the world and see for ourselves the functioning of Dharma.

By taking refuge in the Sangha, we are able to find comfort and support in our friends on the path of Buddhism. In turn, we can be pillars to provide support to others.

Following the three refuges, we find the three pure precepts. From these precepts flow out all our activity.

Cease from evil.

This is the source of Buddha's action. Evil is an expression of anything that causes suffering to beings. Cease from causing suffering to beings.

Do good.

Practice deeds that promote well-being. Act from a selfless place and promote beneficial actions.

Do good for others.

There is no differentiation between the nature of oneself and of others. By doing good for others, you do good for yourself as well.

The Ten Grave Precepts

Refrain from killing.

Respect all life as the life of Buddha. Don't kill Buddha.

Refrain from stealing.

The mind and its objects are one. Our original nature lacks nothing. Don't take things that are not given.

Refrain from misusing sexuality.

Be faithful in relationships. When there is nothing to desire, we are following the way of Buddha.

Refrain from telling lies.

Delusion is difficult enough in this world; don't add to it with lies.

Refrain from using intoxicants.

Keep the mind clear and bright. Don't be deluded as to the nature of reality.

Refrain from criticizing others.

Worry about your own life and follow the path.

Refrain from self-praise and devaluing others.

Praising yourself adds to your own delusion. Devaluing others is no help to living beings.

Refrain from being greedy with Dharma or wealth.

Give freely and without attachment. One verse of Dharma contains the entire universe. Nothing is missing, so there is nothing to envy.

Refrain from acting in anger.

When we act from only anger without reflecting on our actions, we may do things that we regret, that will cause further suffering to living beings. Then a chain of anger will be created from those whom we have harmed. It is OK to feel angry, just as it is OK to experience any other emotion. Make sure that anger does not lead to more harm.

Refrain from defaming the three treasures of Buddha, Dharma, and Sangha.

Treasure the Buddha, Dharma, and Sangha. Share them openly and freely.

Those are the sixteen bodhisattva precepts. These precepts are followed by priests, laypeople, and lay ordained practitioners of Soto Zen. Keep them close to your heart and use them as a guide to limit suffering in your life and the lives of others. These precepts are formally given to individuals who choose to take them at a ceremony called jukai. Jukai is the confirmation of the practitioner to life as a Buddhist. Leading up to jukai, it is quite common for the student of Zen to sew a rakusu, or miniature version of the priest's o-kesa. The rakusu is worn while in the temple, practicing at home, chanting, and sitting zazen.

The rakusu is a physical reminder to ourselves and others of the Buddha's teachings that we unfold each morning and place on ourselves. Each morning after zazen the practitioner recites the o-kesa verse, placing the rakusu on top of the head with hands in gassho: "How great the robe of liberation, a formless field of merit. Wrapping ourselves in Buddha's teaching, we free all living beings."

Samu: Working Zen

What does practice look like when not doing kinhin, zazen, chanting, or bowing? In Zen practice samu is very important. *Samu* means "working practice." This working practice can take many forms, such as

Doing laundry

Working in the garden

Working in the kitchen

Working in the office or on the computer

These are all very common activities within the practice community, both
every day and during sesshin. Samu takes place between zazen, chanting,
and Dharma lectures. Many practitioners often wonder how they can maintain the feeling of sesshin in their everyday lives when they return home.
One great way to do this is to practice samu. Samu is inclusive of all life's
tasks. Think of samu as working meditation, a way to do zazen anytime and
everywhere. No matter what kind of job you are doing, you can practice
samu. Samu can be taking care of your children, working in the office, gro-
cery shopping, taking care of a loved one, or really, anything done with the
intention of practicing the Buddha Way and helping all living beings. When
we work with this attitude, then every weed we pull in the garden or every
email we send can become an act of rooting out our own ignorance and
communicating respectfully.

The key is to look at your task as the most important thing. Try not to think of samu as work. It is not something that needs to be completed, but something you are doing as a means of practice. When you finish a task that is assigned to you during samu practice, you will be given another task to work on, so work just keeps coming your way. Work is never completed, just like our lives from moment to moment—there is always the next job to be done. In a way this is similar to periods of zazen. When we are sitting and really want the bell to ring so we can stand up, do kinhin, stretch, or just think of something fun, inevitably we will have to sit back down to do zazen again.

So, it is best to give up the idea that we will finish, gain anything, or be at some point in time when we don't have to practice anymore. After Shakyamuni Buddha attained enlightenment, he never stopped practicing the way.

There is never a time when Zen practice is separate from enlightenment. Nor a time when enlightenment is separate from practice.

The life of a buddha is practice, and practice is inseparable from enlightenment. Practice does not take place only in a monastery. Practice takes place right where you are. Practice is being a parent when you are parenting, changing diapers, feeding your children, cleaning their clothes, buying them toys, and playing tag. Zen practice is about being in your very life, not about an ancient story that takes place in a far-off time where all conditions for practice are perfect. The conditions of your life are the perfect conditions for practice.

About the Author

Seigaku Amato is a writer, illustrator, and Soto Zen Buddhist priest registered with the Soto-Shu of Japan and is an assistant minister at Long Beach Buddhist Church. His work has been published in *Tricycle: The Buddhist Review, Buddhadharma,* and New World Library publications. Seigaku works full-time polishing the rough edges of his personality, which is a never-ending job. Read more at www.seigakuamato.com.

What to Read Next
from Wisdom Publications

Hardcore Zen

Punk Rock, Monster Movies, and the Truth About Reality

Brad Warner

"*Hardcore Zen* is to Buddhism what the Ramones were to rock and roll: A clear-cut, no-bulls**t offering of truth."
—Miguel Chen, Teenage Bottlerocket

Saltwater Buddha

A Surfer's Quest to Find Zen on the Sea

Jaimal Yogis

"Heartfelt, honest, and deceptively simple. It's great stuff with the words 'Cult Classic' stamped all over it."
—Alex Wade, author of *Surf Nation*

Zen Master Raven

The Teachings of a Wise Old Bird

Robert Aitken

"A new koan anthology that reflects the distinct flavor of American Zen Buddhist practice. This is a beautiful and worthy final teaching from Aitken."
—*Publishers Weekly*

The Dharma of Star Wars

Matthew Bortolin

"A must-read for anyone ever inspired by the wisdom of Yoda, the courage of Luke Skywalker, or even the dark side of Darth Vader."
—Noah Levine, author of *Dharma Punx*

Zen Vows for Daily Life
Robert Aitken

"Robert Aitken Roshi is a poet who deeply appreciates practicing with these gathas. He offers us many beautiful verses, sterling examples of this practice, that we can use to reflect more deeply on what we are doing. I am grateful to Aitken Roshi for offering us this beautiful book."
—from the foreword by Thich Nhat Hanh

I Wanna Be Well
How a Punk Found Peace and You Can Too
Miguel Chen with Rod Meade Sperry

"Much in the spirit of *Dharma Punx, Get in the Van,* or even *Please Kill Me,* Miguel Chen has done something important with this book. And I'm gonna stop feeling self-conscious about listening to DRI while doing yoga."
—Zach Blair, guitarist for Rise Against

The Death of You
A Book for Anyone Who Might Not Live Forever
Miguel Chen

"With a cheerful balance of reverence and irreverence, this book is a joy to read—and Miguel is such a good teacher."
—Cyndi Lee, author of *Yoga Body, Buddha Mind*

About Wisdom Publications

Wisdom Publications is the leading publisher of classic and contemporary Buddhist books and practical works on mindfulness. To learn more about us or to explore our other books, please visit our website at wisdomexperience.org or contact us at the address below.

Wisdom Publications
199 Elm Street
Somerville, MA 02144 USA

We are a 501(c)(3) organization, and donations in support of our mission are tax deductible.

Wisdom Publications is affiliated with the Foundation for the Preservation of the Mahayana Tradition (FPMT).